Havanese Dogs as Pets

A Complete Havanese Owner's Guide

Havanese breeding, where to buy, types, care, temperament, cost, health, showing, grooming, diet, training, and much more included!

By: Lolly Brown

Foreword

Ever wondered about those tiny, cuddly, irresistibly cute little toy dogs that are always sweet and cheerful? Let me introduce you to the Havanese - Cuba's national dog, and a breed that is quickly becoming a favorite among pet owners today.

If you're thinking that there must be a catch - that lovable expression and cheerful temperament cannot possibly be genuine - then the Havanese will quickly prove you wrong. At least, provided there has been proper socialization, and provided that the owner knows the peculiar nuances of caring for a Havanese, this tiny dog will quickly become the clownish and cheerful mainstay of your family.

If you have been considering adding a Havanese to your household, then this book contains useful information, tips and guidelines on the Havanese breed and how to care for them. Enjoy reading!

Table of Contents

Introduction

Havanese dogs are a subtype of Bichon dogs, one of the many toy dogs that developed during the European occupation of the Mediterranean area. Havanese are Cuba's national dog, and while they were originally brought there by Spanish settlers and aristocrats, they certainly developed and adapted to the Cuban landscape and weather to become the breed we know and love today.

Have you been wondering whether a Havanese is the right breed for you? This book contains general information, tips, guidelines and advice on many of the questions you may be asking as you consider adding a Havanese to your household. Within these pages, you will also find information regarding what you will need to know about caring for a Havanese, including nutrient requirements, exercise, and grooming a Havanese. There is also a section on breeding Havanese, as well as on showing Havanese, should these areas be of particular interest to you.

Read on and discover more about the peculiar quirks and traits of this delightful, lovable, and beautiful breed!

Glossary of Dog Terms

AKC – American Kennel Club, the largest purebred dog registry in the United States

Almond Eye – Referring to an elongated eye shape rather than a rounded shape

Apple Head – A round-shaped skull

Balance – A show term referring to all of the parts of the dog, both moving and standing, which produce a harmonious image

Beard – Long, thick hair on the dog's underjaw

Best in Show – An award given to the only undefeated dog left standing at the end of judging

Bitch – A female dog

Bite – The position of the upper and lower teeth when the dog's jaws are closed; positions include level, undershot, scissors, or overshot

Blaze – A white stripe running down the center of the face between the eyes

Board – To house, feed, and care for a dog for a fee

Breed – A domestic race of dogs having a common gene pool and characterized appearance/function

Breed Standard – A published document describing the look, movement, and behavior of the perfect specimen of a particular breed

Buff – An off-white to gold coloring

Clip – A method of trimming the coat in some breeds

Coat – The hair covering of a dog; some breeds have two coats, and outer coat and undercoat; also known as a double coat. Examples of breeds with double coats include German Shepherd, Siberian Husky, Akita, etc.

Condition – The health of the dog as shown by its skin, coat, behavior, and general appearance

Crate – A container used to house and transport dogs; also called a cage or kennel

Crossbreed (Hybrid) – A dog having a sire and dam of two different breeds; cannot be registered with the AKC

Dam (bitch) – The female parent of a dog;

Dock – To shorten the tail of a dog by surgically removing the end part of the tail.

Double Coat – Having an outer weather-resistant coat and a soft, waterproof coat for warmth; see above.

Drop Ear – An ear in which the tip of the ear folds over and hangs down; not prick or erect

Entropion – A genetic disorder resulting in the upper or lower eyelid turning in

Fancier – A person who is especially interested in a particular breed or dog sport

Fawn – A red-yellow hue of brown

Feathering – A long fringe of hair on the ears, tail, legs, or body of a dog

Groom – To brush, trim, comb or otherwise make a dog's coat neat in appearance

Heel – To command a dog to stay close by its owner's side

Hip Dysplasia – A condition characterized by the abnormal formation of the hip joint

Inbreeding – The breeding of two closely related dogs of one breed

Kennel – A building or enclosure where dogs are kept

Litter – A group of puppies born at one time

Markings – A contrasting color or pattern on a dog's coat

Mask – Dark shading on the dog's foreface

Mate – To breed a dog and a bitch

Neuter – To castrate a male dog or spay a female dog

Pads – The tough, shock-absorbent skin on the bottom of a dog's foot

Parti-Color – A coloration of a dog's coat consisting of two or more definite, well-broken colors; one of the colors must be white

Pedigree – The written record of a dog's genealogy going back three generations or more

Pied – A coloration on a dog consisting of patches of white and another color

Prick Ear – Ear that is carried erect, usually pointed at the tip of the ear

Puppy – A dog under 12 months of age

Purebred – A dog whose sire and dam belong to the same breed and who are of unmixed descent

Saddle – Colored markings in the shape of a saddle over the back; colors may vary

Shedding – The natural process whereby old hair falls off the dog's body as it is replaced by new hair growth.

Sire – The male parent of a dog

Smooth Coat – Short hair that is close-lying

Spay – The surgery to remove a female dog's ovaries, rendering her incapable of breeding

Trim – To groom a dog's coat by plucking or clipping

Undercoat – The soft, short coat typically concealed by a longer outer coat

Wean – The process through which puppies transition from subsisting on their mother's milk to eating solid food

Whelping – The act of birthing a litter of puppies

Chapter One: Understanding Havanese Dogs

It is always a good idea to know what you're getting into before you commit to a lifetime companion for the next 12 to 14 years. You might say that it is just a dog, but the Havanese will surely disagree with you. Once you bring him home, he will definitely consider himself a member of your family!

That is really not so bad. Havanese are gentle, loving and affectionate dogs that - while they may be a little shy - are pretty amiable and get along well with everyone. They also love playing with children, so they make good family pets. They are a pretty robust breed, and they will certainly enjoy being the center of attention with their circus-like antics. Though because of their small size, care should certainly be taken during games and playing that they are not injured.

Havanese do not require much room, and neither do they require much exercise. They do, however, require extensive grooming. Their long, silky coat does not stay that way if you leave it alone. If you are set on bringing home a Havanese, then you should be ready to devote the proper attention and investment into their grooming. Their unique coat is pretty high maintenance, and unless you want to see him end up with matted or tangled hair, you will certainly have to be on top of his regular grooming.

Training and obedience lessons are also a good idea for this breed. The Havanese is a clever and intelligent dog, and it behooves owners to recognize that intelligence by giving them a mentally challenging and stimulating environment. Plus, it would certainly be a shame to see a Havanese capable of learning so many tricks and commands but are unable to do so because they were not given the opportunity to learn. Trainings really shouldn't be that difficult anyway - you'll probably be surprised at how quickly they pick up on things. Done right, and in the positive environment, these training and playing sessions, along with their regular grooming, can be perfect bonding experiences between you and your Havanese.

Summary of Havanese Facts

Pedigree: Bichon Tenerife, *Blanquito de la Habana* ("little white dog of Havana"), Poodle, Barbet

AKC Group: Toy Group

Types: no distinction

Breed Size: small

Height: 23-27 cm (9-11 inches)

Weight: 7-14 lbs (3-6 kg)

Coat Length: Long, slightly wavy, profuse and undulating, ranging from 6-8 inches

Coat Texture: very soft double coat, lightweight and silky; in some instances, the undercoat is absent;

Color: all colors possible, including white, cream, fawn, red, chocolate brown, beige, gold, silver, blue, and black, either a solid color or a combination (e.g., sable, brindle, black and tan, tri-color, Irish pied, parti-colored, belton, piebald, black and white, beige black, and white

Eyes and Nose: dark brown eyes with almond-shaped lids surrounded by black pigment; black nose, though chocolate brown dogs may have dark brown pigment on their nose

Ears: dropped and folded ears that can reach halfway to the nose when extended

Tail: arched forward and carried up over its back

Temperament: loyal and attached to their owners, active and lively, very friendly, very sociable, loves to perform in front of others, great need for affection, loves attention, people-oriented, peaceful and gentle

Strangers: friendly even to strangers, though may be a bit shy

Other Dogs: friendly with other dogs

Other Pets: friendly with other pets

Training: very smart and easily trained

Exercise Needs: average, daily exercise can be met with a good game session or a short walk, for about 20-40 minutes a day.

Health Conditions: Luxating patella, liver disease, heart disease, cataracts, retinal dysplasia, tear stains, progressive retinal atrophy, poodle eye, juvenile heritable characters, chonrdodysplasia, leg-calve perthes disease, cardiac, liver and kidney problems, unilateral and bilateral deafness, sebacious adentis, seizures, and dry skin

Lifespan: average 12 to 14 years

Havanese Breed History

The Havanese is part of the Bichon family of dogs, which are all non-sporting companion dog breeds known for their small size, soft and long hair or coat, and amiable dispositions. Many, though not all, of the Bichons come from the Mediterranean, and each are named for their region of origin. The Havanese, in particular, come from Cuba, and is now officially recognized as the national dog of Cuba, whose capital is, of course Havana.

But Bichons are known as an "old world" breed, and they were popular dogs in the courts of medieval Europe, in countries such as France, Italy and Spain. Bichons in general are considered to be descended from the same ancient ancestors of the poodle and the barbet dog breeds. When Spain came to Cuba in 1492, colonization ensued in the next few hundred years, during which settlers came by ship to this tropical island, and they brought with them their pet dogs.

There are still some existing ships' logs of the ships that sailed to Cuba in the early sixteenth century, and dogs were indeed shown to have made the voyage across the seas. Some of those who came to Cuba then were the "segundos," or the second sons of the Spanish aristocracy, and it is theorized that the dogs they brought with them were the

Tenerife - a now extinct dog breed that is considered to be a common ancestor of all Bichon breeds.

These little dogs were soon part of the homes of the resident Spanish aristocracy in Cuba, and the breed evolved and adapted to the new climate, with a very heat-tolerant and lightweight coat. The original settlers called these little white dogs the *Blanquito de la Habana,* or the "little white dog of Havana." Crossbreeding with other Bichon types, perhaps even the poodle, resulted in the modern Havanese, with its wider range of coat colors. They were also called by other names, such as the Havana Silk Dog and the Spanish Silk Poodle.

Many of the European aristocracy who came to Cuba admired this breed, and they were brought back to Europe where they became quite a hit in the courts of Spain, France and England, where they were called "the white Cuban." Queen Victoria and Charles Dickens were among those who had Havanese dogs, and even then they were already being exhibited in the early European dog shows.

Back in Cuba, revolution was brimming, and the bourgeoisie were rising to replace the aristocracy of the sugar barons. The adaptable little Havanese were no longer exclusive to the aristocracy, but have become popular family dogs, even to this day, eventually attaining the nomenclature of the national dog of Cuba.

Of those who fled Cuba during the revolution, some were upper-class Cubans, many of whom came to the United States. The US gene pool then was only 11 little immigrant dogs, and they account for all the Havanese in the world today, except for those who remained in Cuba, and those from the "iron curtain" countries.

The breed was officially recognized by the AKC in 1996, and is now quickly rising in popularity in the United States and the entire world.

Chapter Two: Things to Know Before Getting a Havanese

It is always a good idea to know what you're getting into before you purchase or acquire a dog - whether a Havanese or any other dog breed. All dogs are similar in their need for a good home, good diet and nutrition, proper grooming, training and exercise, but each breed does have its unique and peculiar needs.

To be able to provide a good home for a Havanese, you have to know the quirks and particular needs of this breed, and what it entails to care for one. Then you need to have an honest look at yourself and assess whether you are capable of giving the kind of time, energy and care that a Havanese will need.

Needless to say, the cost of keeping one should also come into play - cutting corners, especially when it comes to food - is never a good idea, especially for a toy breed like the Havanese. Make sure that you can afford its upkeep and the daily nurturing, grooming and training of this breed before you actually bring one home.

This chapter contains some of the more practical concerns that you would need to know before adding a Havanese to your family.

Do You Need a License?

Some states do require you to get a license for dog ownership, while others don't. It depends on the local laws of the region where you live. On the other hand, it is always a good idea to get a license, regardless of whether you are required to or not. Doing so gives you the benefit of legally-recognized ownership.

Be aware that licensing regulations usually come with a rabies vaccination requirement. But since it is necessary for your Havanse to get a rabies vaccination anyway, this isn't an unnecessary burden. Most licenses expire at the end of one year, after which a renewal requires the same proof of rabies vaccination, so it might be said that the two go together.

Once licensed, you will receive the proper documentation, as well as I.D. tags for your Havanese, which you can attach to its collar. In this way, should your Havanese ever become lost, it would be easier for people to trace its ownership back to you. In many ways, complying with licensing regulations protect the public just as much as it protects you and your pet.

How Many Havanese Dogs Should You Keep?

The choice of whether or not to keep one Havanese is really an individual one. As long as you can afford it, have the space, the time and the energy to devote to caring for two toy dogs, then it really only becomes a matter of everyone getting along once everyone has settled in. Be aware that Havanese dogs do require a fair amount of daily grooming, care and attention - not unlike that which you would devote to a child. Having more than one Havanese at a time would therefore be like having more than one child to take care of.

In general, Havanese dogs are pretty mild-mannered and gentle, and so will get along fairly well with other dogs or pets, and that includes other Havanese. Of course, all individual Havanese are unique, and yours might have a particular quirk, especially when it comes to dealing with other humans and other pets. In general though, Havanese prefer the company of humans to other pets. They consider themselves a part of their family, and will be very devoted and attached to their particular owners. This means that they might still want to follow you around to catch your attention, regardless of how many other playmates he has in the house.

On the other hand, having more than one Havanese can also be an advantage by giving you a little time out from Havanese socializing. They dislike solitude and being left alone for long periods of time, and they certainly do not appreciate being ignored for too long. If they have another Havanese to keep them company, then their attention can be divided to allow you some "me-time," as well.

Please always remember that if you do not intend to breed your Havanese, and you intend on keeping a male and female together in the same house, do the responsible thing and have them neutered and spayed early on. Doing so before the female's first heat can actually help her state of health because it lessens the chances of her contracting certain illnesses or diseases. And of course, with dogs being dogs, you might not appreciate being surprised by the Havanese girl one day just turning out to be pregnant!

Do Havanese Dogs Get Along with Other Pets?

Havanese dogs pretty much get along well with everyone, including other pets. They have a gentle and playful temperament, and are very affectionate by nature.

This assumes, however, that your Havanese has been properly socialized. Some representatives of the breed to tend to show moments of shyness, but with proper socialization and a good and positive introduction to all the members of your family, they should be able to develop calm confidence instead of timidity or shyness.

How Much Does it Cost to Keep a Havanese?

Expect the initial costs Havanese ownership to be more expensive during the first year. Aside from the purchase price, vaccination costs, spaying or neutering, and other veterinarian or medical costs. There will also be, of course, the initial purchase of the necessary dog accessories such as a crate or dog bed, food and water bowls, a leash and collar, an assortment of various dog toys, and grooming supplies and equipment.

Below is a table showing a brief overview of the initial expenses of a Havanese dog for the first year.

Initial Cost for a Havanese Dog for the First Year	
Purchase Price	$1,000 - 1,500
Vaccination costs	$50-100
Spaying/Neutering	$150-200
Dog accessories such as a crate, toys, and grooming supplies	$200 and upwards

Remember that the amounts set up above are just estimates, and can vary depending on many factors. Though be aware that the cost of pet supplies and accessories can quickly escalate, especially with a toy dog like the Havanese and the myriad kinds and brands of accessories and grooming supplies that are now commercially available.

But these initial costs still do not factor in the yearly costs of food and supplements, training and obedience classes, grooming costs, and veterinarian exams. You might be able to cut some corners here, especially if you intend to train and groom your Havanese yourself. In general though, here is a brief overview of expected yearly costs for your Havanese:

Annual Cost for a Havanese Dog	
Food, Treats, and Supplements	$650
Training and grooming costs	$230-250
Veterinary exams and checkups	$120-150

Again, these are only estimates, and the amounts can still vary. For your initial year, expect to spend about $1,500 and upwards for your Havanese dog, though this should decrease after the first year to about $750 to $,1000.

What are the Pros and Cons of Havanese Dogs?

Here is a quick run-down of the pros and cons of the Havanese breed. It quickly summarizes many of the salient points you might find important as you consider whether or not this is the right breed for you.

Pros for the Havanese Breed

- Gentle, affectionate, loyal, and good companion pets
- Do not require much room so are ideal for apartments and places that have no yard
- Do not require much exercise since a brief walk or playtime of about 20 minutes each day is usually sufficient
- This is a sturdy breed, and health conditions - though they do exist - are not so prevalent
- They are not "yappy" dogs - though they will bark now and then to give alarms or to alert you when there is someone at the door, for instance; they are mostly quiet dogs
- They are pretty friendly with everyone - including kids and other pets - so they make wonderful family pets
- They are very intelligent and trainable, and love to learn new tricks

Cons for the Havanese Breed

- Their long, silky coat does require extensive maintenance, so you will probably have to invest in quality grooming supplies, and be able to devote a good portion of your time on grooming them.
- This is a breed that does not like being left alone for long periods of time. If you are often away from the house, then this is probably not the right breed for you.
- There are those who say that toy breeds such as the Havanese are difficult to housebreak. Some trainers claim that they are no more so than other breeds. But Havanese do seem to have a stubborn streak, and it can very well manifest in a difficulty to house train.
- You will probably have to pick out the quality dog food brands, which are likely to be more expensive. This is not really a breed with which you can get away with cheaper food.

Chapter Three: Purchasing Your Havanese

After being acquainted with some of the basic facts about Havanese dogs and some of the more practical aspects of what it means to have a Havanese dog and you still feel that this is the breed for you, it is time for you to consider where to get your new family member.

Where Can You Buy Havanese Dogs?

Some might think that a simple trip to the nearest pet shop is the easiest solution, but not necessarily. Unless you're adopting from a rescue, the AKC recommends purchasing your Havanese puppy from a reputable breeder. Otherwise, this might encourage those so-called "puppy mills" who breed indiscriminately and without regard for the health of the sire and dam, or the puppies. Getting a puppy from a reputable breeder also allows you to inquire into the medical history of both the parents and the puppies, which can greatly reduce the chances of your getting a puppy with any congenital health conditions. Doing so also reduces the chances of homeless puppies and dogs, as well as reduce the propagation of Havanese dogs with inherited diseases who would also likely pass these diseases on to their offspring.

Many Havanese - and other canine breed - lovers always advocate breeding for the improvement of the breed. Purchasing from reputable breeders - though it can be considerably more expensive - would be your part in promoting the welfare of the breed as a whole.

Another alternative - and a considerably more humane one - is opening up your home to some of the rescued Havanese Dogs who are only looking for a home to call their own. Granted that there may not be many Havanese rescues near your area - but they do exist. And somewhere out there may be an adult Havanese still waiting to be taken into someone's home.

Here are a few online resources to help you start your search:

United States Rescues:

Havanese Rescue Inc. <http://havaneserescue.com/>

Havanese Angel League Organization (HALO). **<http://www.rescuedhavanese.org/>**

United Kingdom Rescues:

Havanese Club of Great Britain Rescue, as posted on <http://www.thekennelclub.org.uk/services/public/findaresc ue/Default.aspx?breed=6254>

Canadian Rescues

Havanese Fanciers of Canada Rescue. <http://havaneserescue.ca/>

Happy Tails Rescue. <http://www.happytailsrescue.ca/>

How to Choose a Reputable Havanese Breeder

There are many who claim to be reputable Havanese breeders, and yet how can you tell? The decision is yours of course, but discernment in this regard can entail both resourceful networking and proper selectivity. You can usually find a listing of reputable breeders published by your local kennel club - these breeders usually go through a screening process and regular visitations and checkups, so you can at least be assured that they keep on top of their game. Then the more practical thing you could do is to choose the breeder closest to your area, contact him and begin making your inquiries.

If you find yourself choosing between two reputable breeders, then the final decision can really be a personal one. Here are a few guidelines and tips to keep in mind as you make your selection:

- Do your research. Ask around, research about the breed, and about the breeder's history. It might not be such a bad idea to contact some of those Havanese owners who had purchased puppies from this breeder. A good place to network is at your local kennel club - during shows, meetings and gatherings. You'll find yourself in good company, with people who won't mind you asking questions about

Havanese dogs and reputable breeders - they'll probably enjoy discussing it with you!

- Don't be afraid to ask questions of the breeder. A reputable breeder is proud of his puppies, his breeding stock, the lineage of his Havanese dogs, and his breeding site. He should be happy to answer all questions you may have regarding the dam and the sire, and should even be willing to show you the puppies and the site where they are kept.

- Be frank about the pros and cons of this breed, as well as your capacity to care for a Havanese puppy. The breeder is just as interested in seeing his puppies placed in a good home as you are in making sure that this is the right breed for you. The discussion shouldn't mainly be about the cost, but about the best interests of all parties concerned - especially the Havanese puppy!

- Observe. Look around the breeding site. Is it clean and are the puppies well provided for? Notice how the breeder interacts with the puppies and the dam - there should be genuine affection there; reputable breeders are reputable breeders because they care about the breed. They will not be doing it for the money.

- Pay attention to the dogs themselves. Does the mother look healthy and is she nursing all her puppies well? Are the newborn pups active and lively, open to appropriate socialization with each other and the breeder? Are the entire family well provided for, in a comfortable and nourishing environment?

- Here are a few more questions you can ask the breeder: How frequently does the dam give birth to a litter? When was the last litter weaned, and how have they all turned out? Is there any medical history of either the dam or the sire? Are both parents medically certified? How old are they? Do either or both parents come from show dog lineage?

You can probably think of a lot more questions to ask your breeder, and the answers to your questions will go a long way to assuring you that you are making a worthwhile purchase.

Be prepared to answer any questions propounded to you also. Make sure you have done your background work, and are fully set and committed to having a Havanese to care for and be part of your family. The breeder will probably be just as interested in your knowledge and experience of the breed as you are about his.

Finally, ask about the details - will he require a deposit? Will you be allowed to choose a puppy? How much will it cost? When will the pups be weaned? What vaccinations will they be given, and what vaccinations will they still need? What puppy food does the breeder recommend, and in what portions? What are his recommendations regarding exercise, grooming, and training?

Finally, pay a deposit if this is required, and settle down for the wait.

Tips for Selecting a Healthy Havanese Puppy

Yes, all those little puppies in the litter are so cute that you might be tempted to bring them all home. How do you pick? And how do you know that you're making the right choice?

The first thing to remember is that, if you are purchasing your Havanese puppy from a reputable breeder, you can pretty much rest assured that all the puppies in that litter are in the same boat when it comes to health and fitness. This is one of the advantages of doing your groundwork in finding the right breeder. Then it won't be a matter of picking which looks the least sick; you can make your choice based on which little pup appeals to you the most.

You can pick out the one that seems the largest and most dominant, or you can pick out the one that seems most shy. You can choose whether your puppy is a male or a female, or whether it is the one that looks the most like a clown. The choice is freely yours to make. And because this Havanese will be part of your life for the next 12 to 14 years, it is just as important to pick the one with whom you seem to have good chemistry, as it is to pick one in good overall health.

In general, though, there are certain signs and responses you can recognize that shows a healthy puppy, and which you can use as a gauge to make your selection:

- Good responsiveness to your presence - following your finger as you move it, for instance, responsiveness to the sound of your voice, and a certain openness to the presence of strangers.

- Look at the pup's general state of health: are the eyes clear and free of discharges? Is he active and responsive during feeding time? Is the coat shiny and healthy-looking? Does he respond appropriately to noise, voices, sounds? Does he seem curious about you?

Puppy-Proofing Your Home

Once you have purchased your Havanese puppy, it is time to bring him home. But before you do that, you need to puppy-proof your home.

Although for toy breeds like the Havanese, it isn't just puppy-proofing, but Havanese-proofing. This tiny breed is mostly an indoor breed, which means that he will be spending most of his time indoors. And while they may eventually grown out of the playful and curious puppy stage of getting into all sorts of trouble, it is best to exercise due caution even when your little Havanese puppy has "grown." Being constantly in the house, even if he has a crate, the chances are good that he will eventually have access to pretty much all the rooms in your house at one point or another.

This is especially true for this companion breed that hates being separated from his owners for long. The dangers posed by the same household items will continue to pose a constant danger even to grown-up Havanese dogs.

There are a great number of seemingly harmless household items that may be dangerous to leave where they are once you bring your puppy home. There are those who actually recommend that you get down on your hands and knees and explore your house from this unique vantage point, trying to see things the way a four-legged tiny dog would see things. Certain household items may already have caught your eye as things that could pose some danger to your Havanese - if so, secure them, or put them away somewhere safe.

Havanese are generally mind-mannered and obedient dogs, but they do have a curious and playful nature, and like most pups, are almost certain to follow their nose and their inclination to chew. Here are a few household things you might watch out for as you go around puppy-proofing your home for the arrival of its newest member:

- Remove all toxic plants from the floor. If you don't know which are toxic, it is probably best to remove all plants from within your Havanese's reach until you've had a chance to make sure.
- Keep all small items safely organized and stored. You can offer your Havanese their new and expensive chew toys, but their curiosity will certainly lead them to want to explore other things. Dogs of most breeds are notorious for putting things in their mouths, chewing things, or even swallowing them. Small items left lying around may prove to be the cause for an emergency trip to the hospital!
- Store all household cleaners, medicines, food, and other similar items up off the ground, preferably in a high place. The same is also true for the garbage or

the trash can. Open sources of water should also be sealed securely, as well as open sources of fire.

- Don't allow tablecloths or long curtains to trail to the floor. There might be a temptation to pull on something that is hanging so invitingly, which could result in ruined curtains and cloths, not to mention all that can fall off of the table.

- Be particularly careful of hanging cords and electrical cables - aside from the danger of possible strangling, chewing on electrical cables could also cause unfortunate electrocution. In the same vein, cover up all electrical outlets or sockets that are near the floor.

- If you have a yard and allow your Havanese free rein, don't forget to fence in the yard all around so that he will not wander around and make his way to the streets. Also make sure that there are no toxic plants or grass that your Havanese might chew on. Havanese are not generally wanderers, but one can never tell, and it is always best to exercise proper caution.

- Be particularly careful of the fencing around your yard, or the balconies and stairs. This is a very small breed, and they can certainly fit in between what might seem like reasonably narrow slots. You might think of installing screens or a mess fence to keep them safe.

- If registered and duly licensed, make sure that they are wearing their collar and ID tags at all times. If he ever does get lost, this will enable others to help him find his way back to you as quickly as possible.

Chapter Four: Caring for Your New Havanese

And now begins what could possibly be a very beautiful friendship - if you do it right. This chapter and those following contains some general guidelines and information on caring for your Havanese. For now, let's look at what makes an optimal living space for your Havanese, and the daily exercise requirements they would need.

Ideal Habitat Requirements for your Havanese

The good news is that Havanese don't take up much space - as you can easily surmise from their tiny size. They are indoor pets, and they were bred to be companion pets, so they'll pretty much stick as close to you as possible whenever you're home. Some Havanese have even been known to grab a mouthful of food from their bowl, follow you where you're sitting on the couch, drop the food on the floor and proceed to eat right in front of you. It's because they prefer being in your company to being anywhere else.

That is why it is not a good idea to leave Havanese alone in the house for long periods of time. This is a breed that does not do well in isolation. They thrive on company, and they are always pleased to be the center of anyone's attention. They are friendly and loving dogs, which means that they will also prefer being in the company of those on whom they can shower their affection and perform tricks for. All this aside from the fact that if you own a Havanese, you are responsible for frequent grooming sessions to keep their coats in good order. Therefore, if your lifestyle keeps you out of the house for long periods of time, or keeps you busy so that you have no time or opportunity to devote to the grooming and exercise of your Havanese, then this breed is probably not right for you.

That said, Havanese do not really need much room. They can do well in small spaces and are quite apartment-friendly, as long as they get enough daily exercise. There were some Havanese who have been used as herders in Cuba, so they do enjoy the occasional spurts of running and playing on fields and wide open spaces, their very versatility allows them to expend their energy on a number of different exercises, some of which can be done indoors or within limited space.

Be sure to provide them with a crate or, if you prefer a dog bed, make sure you have a temporary gated-off living space, especially if they have not yet been housebroken. Here are some other accessories and equipment you should have ready for the use of your Havanese:

- Food and water bowls
- Leash and collar
- Toys, particularly chew toys
- Low baby gates which you can use to secure portions of your house

Exercise Requirements for Havanese Dogs

Again, a good news is that Havanese doesn't need much exercise. Though they are a very energetic breed - and they can certainly surprise you with their occasional bursts of high energy and activity, because they also consume energy faster than larger dogs, short periods of daily exercise is usually sufficient.

You could take them for daily walks of about twenty minutes each day, or playtime for about the same amount of time - whether indoors or outdoors, is usually enough to satisfy their exercise requirements.

While you can start with a ballpark time of about twenty minutes, it is always best to adjust depending on your particular Havanese's unique needs. You can usually tell, simply by paying attention, whether or not their daily exercise is too much or too little. A Havanese that is getting sufficient daily exercise will be a calm and contented dog at home. Too little exercise could easily translate to destructive behavior such as chewing destroying property; on the other hand, a listless and lethargic Havanese might mean that he is being given too much exercise than he can handle. Pay attention. There is no standard answer to all pets, but while there are guides and tips for your daily activities, each must always be adjusted according to the unique needs of each dog.

Chapter Five: Meeting Your Havanese Dog's Nutritional Needs

There are many brands of commercially-available dog food these days, and there are even some which are breed-specific; i.e., "specially-formulated Havanese dog food." But how do you know which is good dog food, or which is at least better than others? Feeding Havanese dogs, in particular, can be a genuine concern for many owners - as they might tend to notice their Havanese eating sparingly and leaving too many leftovers in the bowl too often. Naturally you want your dog to be in good health, and the cornerstone of that is what you feed them. This chapter explores some of the basics of canine nutrition in general, and on the peculiar quirks of feeding Havanese dogs in particular.

The Nutritional Needs of Dogs

That "specially-formulated" dog food is labeled so because it is intended to supply the nutritional needs of dogs. It's a bit similar to how we humans also need essential nutrients, vitamins and minerals in our diet to aid in our biological processes and metabolism. For dogs, here are some of the essential nutrients that comprise the building blocks of a Havanese's good health, with a short description of each:

Proteins

Mainly obtained from meat and most meat-based products, protein is essential for growth and cell regeneration and repair, and for Havanese, are necessary to help maintain their beautiful long and silky coat. Be aware that experts do not recommend feeding your dog raw eggs, as this may have actually be harmful to their health.

Carbohydrates

This is usually derived from fiber-based products, and help in maintaining the intestinal health of your pet.

Some carbohydrates can even be a good source of energy for your pet.

Fats

Fats provide your pet with a concentrated source of energy, and are also essential for some vitamins (A, E, D and K) to be absorbed. They help in protecting the internal organs and are vital in cellular production.

Vitamins and Minerals

Vitamins and minerals usually cannot be synthesized by a dog's body, so the primary source of these are the synthesized versions obtainable in commercially available quality dog foods. Vitamins and minerals help in the normal functioning of their bodies, and also helps maintain their bones and teeth.

Water

Water must, of course, not be forgotten. Just like humans, about 60 to 70 percent of a dog's body weight is comprised of water, and he will have to replenish this often as he loses it. Clean water must always be available to your Havanese; loss of water in the body can certainly cause illness, and severe dehydration can be fatal.

How to Select a High-Quality Dog Food Brand

The choice of which dog food brand to select for your Havanese is always a personal one, and you may have to try several different brands before you pick the right one that supports and satisfies your Havanese's health needs and unique feeding quirks. Here are a few guidelines to help you, however, in making an informed choice:

- Select a small breed dog food. While Havanese can pretty much eat most quality dog food, small breeds like the Havanese are more active, have faster metabolism, and tend to burn energy faster compared to large and medium breeds. Small breed dog foods are usually formulated with more calories to help provide your Havanese the energy it needs. Small breed dog foods are also more dense in terms of calories and nutrients. This is because it factors in the smaller stomachs of toy breeds, who would certainly need the same nutrient amounts in smaller bites.
- Read the label. Steer clear of artifical flavors, colors, sweeteners and preservatives.
- Most experts recommend selecting dog food whose first three ingredients are meat-based. The main ingredients in most dog food are protein and fats, and you can usually identify the source in the first few

ingredients listed on the label. The first few ingredients on the label of all dog foods comprise the greatest portion of the dog food component, as they are legally obligated to arrange the comprising ingredients in descending order based on their pre-cooked weights.

- Be inquiring. You might ask your veterinarian what his professional opinion is regarding the best dog food brand for Havanese in particular. And you don't need to stop there. Read a lot, ask around, and most of all, pay attention to the state of health of your Havanese.

Daily Energy Requirements

You've probably heard the term RER before, or Resting Energy Requirements, and are wondering what this could possibly have to do with dog nutrition.

RER is the daily recommended caloric intake of your pet, which is calculated based on his weight. For toy breeds like the Havanese, the formula used is that which is used for dogs weighing between 2 and 45 kg (5-99 lbs.):

RER = 30 (body weight in kilograms) + 70

The result is the daily energy requirement of your pet while he is at rest, and a quick look at your dog food's label to determine the calories per cup should tell you how many cups to give him each day. And yet you might wonder about this very formula itself, which may seem anathema to the Havanese that is a generally active and lively breed. Why would you want to know his daily energy requirement when he is at rest - which he seldom is?

If you thinking along these same lines, then you are on the right track. For while the RER is a good base amount to start with, it is not such a simple thing as a standard portion of food to feed all Havanese of the same weight. Once they start being active, and stops being at rest, the RER adjusts to these additional energy requirements. Aside from their regular daily activities, these variables can also include their life stage - whether a puppy, a mature adult, pregnancy, when they are nursing, or when they have entered their senior years. The temperature and the weather can also have an effect, as is whether your Havanese is neutered or not.

Below is a simple table demonstrating how the RER is adjusted depending on the unique life stage, environment, and lifestyle of your Havanese.

Neutered Adult	RER x 1
Intact Adult	RER x 1.6
Moderate Work Adult	RER x 3
Pregnant dog in the last 21 days before birth	RER x 3
Weaning Puppy	RER x 3
Adolescent Puppy	RER x 2
Obese Puppy undergoing weight loss activities	RER x 1

The obvious implication is that, just as you don't eat the same thing in the same amounts each day, the diet of your Havanese can also vary, sometimes on a daily basis depending on his daily exercise regimen, for example. And don't forget to factor in the treats you give him each day.

Really the best thing for you to do, if you are at all unsure about how best to feed your pet, is always to consult with your veterinarian. Together, you can come up with a feeding schedule that would also factor in your Havanese's current state of health. Using this as a basis, and considering the basic understanding of RER above, you can make little adjustments each day depending on how active your dog has been, or if you see your Havanese growing a bit soft around the tummy.

Never forget though, that you should never make any drastic or major changes in your pet's diet without first consulting your vet.

Tips for Feeding Your Havanese

Obesity is not that big a concern for toy breeds such as the Havanese; in fact, many owners are actually worried that their Havanese may not be getting enough to eat. The breed has been said to be picky eaters, which does seem borne out by the amount of dog food they'll leave untouched in the bowl. And because Havanese are so fond of treats, you'll wonder if they're getting enough of their daily nutrient requirements if the bulk of their daily diet comprise treats.

One way you might train your Havanese out of being picky about their food is to have a set feeding schedule. Instead of leaving dog food in the bowl to sit for hours at a time, clean the bowl after about an hour after his feeding schedule has started. This would teach him that he can only expect to eat his daily dog food at a certain time, and that he should eat it immediately because he cannot leave it to eat for later. Don't overfeed treats either - don't give more than you usually do. But don't forget to give him his dog food at the same time each day, either. Once he begins to learn and adjust to this time-specific schedule and cleanup, you might find it a boon in terms of housebreaking, also!

Dangerous Foods to Avoid

It is especially important to be cautious in feeding Havanese, as they are so often right beside us that there is always a temptation to just reach over and give them a share of what you're eating. But this is not always a good thing to do. For one thing, overfeeding treats can cause obesity, which is currently becoming a serious problem among different dog breeds. For another thing, not all "people-food" are safe for dogs to eat.

Here are some of the foods that are not recommended for canine consumption as they can be outright dangerous to your pet. Should your Havanese ingest any of these ingredients, be sure to call emergency services immediately for assistance.

- Alcohol
- Apple seeds
- Avocado
- Cherry pits
- Chocolate
- Citrus

- Coconut
- Coffee
- Garlic
- Grapes/raisins
- Hops
- Macadamia nuts
- Milk and Dairy
- Mold
- Mushrooms
- Mustard seeds
- Onions/leeks
- Peach pits
- Potato leaves/stems
- Raw meat and eggs
- Rhubarb leaves
- Salty snacks
- Tea
- Tomato leaves/stems
- Walnuts
- Xylitol
- Yeast dough

Chapter Six: Training Your Havanese

As with the training of any other breed, the first few attempts can be very frustrating as you and your Havanese struggle to understand each other. Any Havanese owner must have patience, consistency and dedication, because while this breed does show occasional streaks of stubbornness, they are a highly clever and intelligent breed and will eventually prove the worth of all those training hours you spent with them.

So if you have days of frustration when it seems that your Havanese is not listening to you - just keep at it. If they seem like they would rather do anything other than what you tell them, don't give up. Patience does have its rewards - especially for this breed, who certainly have the capacity to learn a great number of commands, tricks and skills that they'll probably even surprise you!

Socializing Your New Havanese Puppy

Just like any other dog, Havanese training starts with proper socialization. This is an especially crucial time for the Havanese's training, since there might be a tendency to be shy or fearful if not properly socialized. There are some breeders who say that around 8 weeks, even though they are fully weaned (or because of it), the little pups enter a fear stage, and confidence and trust must be built between humans and the puppy before they are separated from their mother.

Socialization begins with the introduction of little things each day, to get them used to the presence of strange and new things while also gradually building up their coping mechanisms. The breeder must have already set the stage with small, daily and gentle handling to get them used to the presence of a human. Once you bring the pup home, it is your turn to continue the socialization process.

You might begin by introducing new things each day - small things around the house are good places to start, especially as these will be things he will have to contend with everyday: the presence of the rest of your household, for instance, especially if you have children, as well as other pets, each can be a supervised introduction. Then there is the introduction to the place where he will be sleeping, such as a crate or a dog bed. There are also the things in the house - the phone ringing, the kettle boiling, the sound of the television, etc. Gradually, you might begin exploring the yard together, introducing him to the feel of a collar and a leash, and eventually, short walks that will progressively get longer as he begins to gain his confidence.

The important thing in this gradual socialization process is to introduce the wider world while also allowing him to adjust gradually, building his confidence the more he begins to explore the world. You do not want him to be afraid or fearful, otherwise he will be living a very stressful life as being in a human household will certainly necessitate constant changes, sights, smells, and sounds. You want him to be confident, while keeping his friendly temperament and sweet disposition. You can do this by making sure that each new experience is done in a positive and cheerful atmosphere.

Crate Training - Housebreaking Your Puppy

There are those who say that Havanese and other toy breeds are difficult to housebreak, but this is no more than true than it is with other breeds. Perhaps it is because of their tiny size and our capacity to carry them that makes housebreaking a bit difficult. That is because effective housebreaking requires clear and constant signals, a regular feeding schedule, and a certain period of confinement.

Pick a crate that is roomy enough for the puppy to move around in. At first, make their stay inside the crate short - provide them with proper cushions or blankets to keep them comfortable, and even some toys to keep them distracted while they are inside. The main thing is to get them familiar with the crate until they no longer being confined within it. If done properly, they may even begin to look at the crate as their own personal space.

If they should go while they are inside the crate, make a disapproving sound, scoop them up quickly and bring them to the yard or the litter box. This enables them to make a quick connection that what you are disapproving of is their going inside the crate. This is opposed to when you only make the disapproving sound after you see the evidence, which could be hours after the fact, in which case your signal might only confuse them if they aren't doing anything wrong right at that moment.

You might want to try bringing him to the yard or the litter box at about the same time the next day, and reward him with praises and even treats when he does his business where he's supposed to. Be patient, be consistent in your signals, and above all, keep to a regular feeding schedule. Once he succeeds on his first try, you might want to begin making his potty schedule standard, too.

Make sure that you clean his crate if you should see such evidence inside - some, not all, Havanese, have been known to eat their own poop - which will certainly not be good for their health.

When they begin learning and keeping to a consistent schedule, then you can gradually allow her a slightly bigger space to explore, while maintaining the same crate confinement and feeding and potty training schedule each day.

Be patient while the little puppy is learning this first lesson. Remember that he wants to please you, so it is up to you to make the lesson as clear as possible. And before you know it, you have a housebroken Havanese!

Some Training Methods for for Obedience Training

Havanese are natural little show-offs - they love attention and praise, and are naturally eager to please. They also excel in agility and circus-like tricks, and are intelligent enough to master a good number of commands. They are so versatile that they have also been put to use as trackers, therapy dogs, and helpers of people with disability - aiding the latter by picking up or fetching items for their owners.

Your very own Havanese might have the makings of a good show dog, or an excellent working dog. If so, it all begins with basic obedience training. There are a few methods that you might try as you begin training your own Havanese:

Positive Reinforcement

Havanese naturally love to please you, their owner, especially if they trust you and have a strong bond with you. So essentially, the way to encourage them during any training session is to use lots of praises and rewards.

Use praises more than you use treats and rewards, for while the occasional treat may be a good motivator, it does not do to have your Havanese pay attention to you only when they can smell that treat in your pocket. For the well-adjusted Havanese, a good praise is motivation enough.

For discouraging unwanted behavior, on the other hand, it is not a good idea to use loud or aggressive sounds to signal your disapproval. After a brief negative expressioin delivered in a firm voice, simply withhold your attention for a brief time. Done consistently enough, and immediately after the unwanted behavior, they would be quick enough to pick up on what you are trying to teach them not to do.

The Clicker Training Method

The use of a clicker is really just a replacement for all the gushing "Good boy!" or "Good girl!" expressions after your Havanese has followed your command. It is a more standardized, distinct, and neutral signal which, if properly taught, will quickly train your Havanese to recognize it as a positive signal.

Essentially, this method advocates using the clicker for each desired behavior, or for each positive response to a command, and each click is immediately followed by a treat. Command - positive response - clicker - treat. Done this way, your Havanese quickly learns what is expected of him, and he may even begin to look forward to those clicking sounds.

Eventually, as each command is given and obeyed, you can begin reducing the amount of the treats, or using treats only for commands that have yet to be learned. The important thing here is that your Havanese learns that the sound of the clicker means he has done something that pleases you. Once he begins to make this connection, the clicker can be used as a standard method for many of the different and myriad commands you wish to teach your Havanese.

As you try to work out which method works best for you and your Havanese, here are a few guidelines you might also remember as you begin training:

- Havanese are very intelligent and clever animals, and have a surprisingly discerning mind. They will quickly pick up a great number of different word commands and the equipment that goes with those commands. But it is always best to do things slowly - start out by teaching them one command at a time. Even if they seem to have mastered the word "Stay!" in one day, it's always best to make sure they remember it by using it often enough for the next two or three days before moving on to the next command. Then the lessons will change; but of course, try to use some of the learned commands regularly, too.
- Be observant as to which trick or training method he prefers. If he seems happy learning how to fetch his

toy for you, for instance, then start with that. It's always best to start out any training in a positive atmosphere, and for the Havanese, with plenty of praise and positive reinforcement. Then he will be more open to learning new things.

- Be careful about the use of treats during training. It is commonly acknowledged that too much treats can cause canine obesity, which you certainly don't want in your beautiful Havanese. Give only small treats - and if it has been a particularly good training period with lots of earned treats, make it up by reduced portions in their regular diet, or a bit more exercise the next day.

- Reinforce the desired behavior, and express your disapproval of the undesired behavior, immediately after it has been committed. Remember that while Havanese cannot speak human language, they will learn to use spoken commands given time. At first, though, they will need to learn what is expected of them and to make the necessary connections and associations. Be patient, and above all, be consistent and clear in your signals. Immediately expressing your approval or disapproval immediately after - or even during - the act helps them identify which behavior you are reacting to. Clear and consistent signals will actually work to your advantage because it speeds up the training process, and assumes the willingness and readiness of your Havanese to learn and to please you. Don't sell your Havanese short. Teach them well, and they'll probably even surprise you with how intelligent they are!

- And lastly, remember that Havanese are a small and somewhat delicate breed, with a friendly and cheerful - sometimes even clownish - nature and temperament. They will not respond well to harsh, aggressive, or violent training methods.

Chapter Seven: Grooming Your Havanese

Whether you keep your Havanese in full coat, or whether you choose to give him one of the many trims and cuts that are popular for the breed, regular grooming is a must. Their trademark long and silky coat needs maintenance and care, and of course overall grooming is necessary to keep your Havanese in top shape and health.

Remember that grooming should take place as early as possible, even if it starts with simple brushing of the coat. The habit of grooming is acquired, and if done in the right atmosphere and with the right care, might even become an enjoyable time for your pet. It can certainly serve as the perfect bonding time for you and your Havanese.

Check out some of the grooming tips below!

Recommended Tools to Have on Hand

- Small and soft slicker brush
- Pin brush
- Comb
- Flea comb
- Conditioner
- Dog toothbrush and toothpaste
- Dog ear cleaner
- Dog shampoo

Tips for Bathing Havanese Dogs

How often should you bathe your Havanese? There is really no right anwer - it depends to a large extent on how active he is, and therefore how often his tendency is to get dirty and smelly. This is especially important for toy breeds like the Havanese who are often on the furniture, and are carried quite close by their owners.

Some are okay with bathing once a month, though for some the frequency can range from once a week to once every two weeks. The good news with toy breeds is that because of their size, bathing can be carried out quite conveniently in the kitchen sink, where the size is more than appropriate for them, and the entire process is also within your reach. Use a quality dog shampoo and conditioner. The conditioner is quite important given the silky feel of the Havanese coat, much like the texture of human hair. You dont want it stripped of its natural oils by using too much shampoo too often.

And don't forget to dry them off completely - start with brisk towel drying, and them finish it off with a small blower at the minimum setting, held about a feet away. Once they are completely dry, finish it off with a good comb and brush.

Tips for Grooming Havanese Dogs

Havanese are minimal shedders. Though some might say that they do not shed, there will be hair and coat coming off at intervals, sometimes in the comb and brush, or on the furniture. And because of the length of their coats, it is extremely important to groom regularly to prevent tangles and matting. You'll learn pretty quick that putting off grooming for a few days or so will only mean more trouble for you in the long run.

It is highly recommended that brushing be done at least once to thrice per week. You can begin by spraying some conditioner or rinse before the brushing process, as it can add a lovely sheen to their coats, and it helps minimize the damage done by dryness and static buildup. You can use an assortment of brushes depending on your choice, though many groomers prefer using a soft pin brush to minimize coat damage and skin irritation.

Despite its small size, you'll probably be surprised at how much hair you'll be dealing with. You can do the brushing in sections or layers, parting a section down to the skin before moving on the others. Go gently and slowly until each section is smooth and without any tangles. You'll probably find the spray-on conditioner to be a big help. Though remember to be careful when you get near the eyes and ears. For the face, the beard and the corners of the eyes, stick to using a comb. Use a spray if you must, but be careful that it doesn't get into your Havanese's eyes, nose, mouth and ears.

Other Grooming Tasks

Trimming the Havanese's Pad and Nails

This will probably not be one of your Havanese's favorite part of the grooming, but if done in the right spirit and with great care, it should not be too difficult. Go slowly, especially for small breeds such as the Havanese where the nails are considerably smaller, and might even be hidden by an abundance of hair.

The reason for taking so much caution is because you might end up cutting the quick - the blood vessel that supplies blood to the nails. If you are a little unsure at first about how to do this, or whether you can, it is better that you let a professional do it - whether a groomer or a Vet - at least at first, just to show you how it's done.

This little hairy toy breed can also have some fuzz growing out between the pads of its little feet. This should be trimmed regularly, not only to keep the feet presentable and safe from slipping on hard surfaces, but also too keep the pads from splaying. Use blunt-nosed clipprs to trim the excess hair between the pads. Again, if you are unsure, have a professional demonstrate this to you - at least at first. You'll probably get the hang of it quite quickly.

Cleaning Your Havenese's Ears

It is imperative that you consult with a professional - whether a vet or a groomer - as to how to handle the cleaning of your Havanese's ears. This is because the amount of hair that can grow inside your dog's ears can vary; some have abundant growth, and some have considerably less. While some do prefer plucking the hair from within the ears, this is certainly not feasible for those with abundant growth of hair inside the ears.

The reason for keeping the inner ears as clean and clear of hair as possible is because the presence of so much hair can be very inviting for the growth of bacteria and infection, especially once moisture is trapped inside and is unable to dry because of the unique shape and fold of the Havanese ears. There are also dog ear cleaning solutions available, to help you clean the inner ears to keep it free of wax and dirt buildup. You should never use a Q-tip for dog's ears, as their ears are very sensitive and a wrong move might cause very real damage.

If this is your first time and you have never cleaned the inside of a Havanese - or any dog's - ears before, it is highly recommended you seek the help and guidance of a professional, at least at first. The ears are not a good place for experimental grooming, so exercise due caution.

Cleaning Your Havanese's Eyes

The abundance of Havanese hair might also cause some discomfort in your pet's eyes. Daily eye cleaning is highly recommended. With a warm facecloth, gently wipe at the corners of your Havanese's eyes, removing any dirt buildup. Many owners use clips and other accessories to keep the hair away from the eyes of their Havanese pets, while others prefer giving their Havanese a good trim. The decision is up to you, as long as you make sure that the eyes of your Havanese are kept clean and healthy.

Brushing Your Havanese's Teeth

There are dog toothrbush and toothpaste specially formulated for canine needs, but if this causes discomfort to your Havanese, you can probably start with a clean moist cloth or your fingers at first - just to get them used to the feel of a foreign object rubbing against their teeth. If you start them when they're young, they will soon grow to realize that there is nothing frightening about having their teeth brushed. They might even grow to enjoy the process.

At first, start out with just the teeth that are within easy reach. Go slowly, and if you only reach the front teeth at first, that's already a pretty good start. Eventually, and with patience, you will reach the backteeth - which you can do by lifting the corner flaps of their lips. Be gentle. Cleaning where you can reach is already a pretty good cleaning session for both you and your Havanese.

Coat Trimming - to Trim or Not to Trim?

The question of whether or not to trim your Havanese's coat is entirely up to you - these days, there are even a great range of various cuts and styles that groomers offer Havanese pet owners. As you decide however, keep these few facts in mind:

- The AKC does not accept Havanese whose coats are trimmed. If you are planning on showing your Havanese, you will have to care for and nurture their long and silky coat regularly, sans the cutting.
- Remember also that the unique silky and lightweight coat of the Havanese was an adaptation of the breed to the tropical climate of Cuba - to protect it from the heat and sun. If you deprive them of too much of this protection and they are subsequently exposed to the elements - whether heat or cold - it could have a serious detrimental effect on their health.
- As with any other dog breed, the Havanese coat is their protection - not only from the weather and the

elements - but also from various parasites, insects, sharp glass blades and other environmental factors that can cause injuries, allergies, wounds, and other skin problems. So while there are some who shave their Havanese down to their skin, this is not recommended. Also keep in mind that trimming the Havanese coat too often might alter or damage the natural silky texture of your pet's coat.

Chapter Eight: Breeding Your Havanese

If you are thinking about breeding your Havanese dogs, take some time and think about whether you even should. Dog breeding is a huge responsibility, and if you are getting into it just so you could make extra money, then be warned that you'll probably be lucky if you come out even. There will be vaccinations, food and boarding of the stud, the mother, and the puppies to consider, testing for possible diseases, and a huge investment of time and energy. Potential Havanese owners will expect you to be there every step of the way.

Many pet owners now are very discriminating in the pets they choose, and as a responsible breeder you should be able to satisfy people's questions, needs, and requirements. Pet lovers are adamant on the motto of breeding for the improvement of the breed, which means eliminating the possibility of genetic conditions and illnesses by not breeding those who have not been given a clean bill of health. You would not want a litter of puppies who have a high chance of developing illnesses, and might even pass it on to their offspring. Of course there is never always a 100% guarantee of good health in your Havanese litter, but you should be able to show that you did the responsible thing all throughout the process.

If you do not think that Havanese breeding is for you, or if your Havanese does have a genetic illness or health condition, then it behooves you to have your pet spayed or neutered. It has been said that spaying or neutering a female dog before her period of first heat might actually eliminate or lower the chances of her contracting certain illnesses or diseases.

If, on the other hand, the health prospects of your Havanese are good, and you are willing to devote the time and energy to becoming a responsible Havanese breeder, this chapter contains some basic information you might find useful on dog breeding. Remember though, that the birth of any new life is always a unique experience, and you will find yourself always learning something new. Use this book as the beginning of your study, or as a supplement. But the learning must never stop.

Basic Dog Breeding Information

Before breeding, make sure you have done your groundwork: a careful selection and medical testing of the dame and stud, and careful preparation for the entire breeding process - from mating, whelping, weaning and raising the puppies, and placing the puppies in their new homes.

Once a stud contract has been finalized, the next thing to do is wait until your female Havanese is ready. Prepare the site where the dog would be kept, and be ready to house both the dam and the stud for at least two weeks or more. When the dam begins showing signs of her cycle, then it is time to get started.

This is the time when the female is considered "in heat." For small dogs, it typically occurs at about six months, maybe sooner, maybe later. It varies, but some of the signs to watch out for are a swollen vulva and some bloody and vaginal discharge. Beware that a female dog in heat has a very distinctive smell that dogs around the area -

particularly male dogs - will notice and respond to. It is also not a good idea to breed your dog during her first heat - she needs physical and psychological maturity to become a mother, so it is best to wait - ideally for her third cycle or later. Ideally, she should not be younger than two years old. Heat cycles in dogs usually occur twice a year, sometimes even three times, so she will be fertile at least twice or three times a year.

The swollen vulva and vaginal discharge are signs that your Havanese is in the first stage of her heat cycle - the proestrus. The female will not accept the male at this time, but it is ideal if there could be some socialization between them. That is why it is important to have the necessary space to house two dogs. You'll probably notice the male sniffing and licking at the female at this time. The proestrus stage usually lasts for about a week or so, and then she enters the estrus stage, at around the seventh to ninth day. The bloody discharge will become watery and will change colors to something a bit more yellow, and at this time she will be ready to accept the male.

Breeding or mating may take about forty-five minutes. The male will mount the female from behind, and after a period of pelvic thrusts, there will be penetration and ejaculation. Once this ceases, the dam and stud will remain connected for about 10 to 30 minutes still while they remain connected rear to rear. This is called the tie, and results from the section of the penis called the bulbus glandis swelling inside the vagina. Don't try to separate them at this time or you risk causing injury to both the male and the female. They will part on their own once they are ready. If one or both of them are new to mating, it is a good idea to be present and keep them from injuring themselves by moving around too much.

Mating may take place once each day after this - until the female stops accepting the male. The most fertile period is during estrus, or around the time that she is most receptive to the male, usually around 10 to14 days.

Basic Dog Pregnancy and Whelping Information

The gestation period lasts for about 58 to 63 days, and while there may be signs that is pregnant during this time, the only way to really be sure is by a verterinary checkup around day 28 to 30. Some dogs only show signs of false pregnancy, and a veterinarian will be able to confirm if the breeding was successful.

Now it's time to set yourself up for the dog's pregnancy and the impending birth, or whelping. It is always a good idea to consult with your Veterinarian regarding his recommendations on diet and exercise for pregnant dogs. You might decrease her exercise regimen a little - especially agility exercises, and discuss a recommended feeding schedule with your vet. Generally, there would be slight increase in food portions towards the latter weeks of the pregnancy.

Your Vet will also be able to give you a possible due date for the birth, though for small breeds like the Havanese, gestation can take longer than most. When the time approaches, you should be notice some nesting behavior in your pregnant Havanese. It is a good idea to have her whelping box prepared beforehand, and to get her accustomed to it after you have confirmed pregnancy. She will probably stay in this box for long periods of time, or she may want to stay closer to you during this time, be more affectionate, and more restive. These are all possible signs of approaching delivery.

Dogs will have experience a drop in their temperatures when they start going into labor - to about 98 from the normal 100 or 101 degrees Fahrenheit. Her temperature will continue to drop, and whelping should take place within the next few hours.

You will notice her shivering, panting, and examing and licking herself. Panting and contractions usually precede the appearance of each puppy.

The Havanese has an average litter of from 1 to 9 puppies, and so the time of whelping and contractions would depend upon the size of the litter. Some dogs can also take long breaks in between puppies, while others will push out their puppies one after another. It varies, so just be sure to be present to support her and encourage her during this time. If there is no sign of the puppies around two hours after the contractions started, you should probably call your Veterinarian. Keep careful records of the time that labor began and the time that the contractions started, for your vet will be sure to ask you these questions.

Each puppy will come with its own placenta, which can either follow the appearance of the pup, or will still encase the newbor pup. Should the latter take place, the mother's instincts should kick in and she will tear this sac open with her teeth and lick the face and nose of the newborn to stimulate breathing. If she does not do this - especially if it is her first time = you should then be ready to step in and do what is necessary. You can tear the sac open yourself, and stimulate breathing by using a rough towel to clear the pup's air passages. If the mother also does not chew through the connecting umbilical cord, you should be able to do this yourself - most recommend using dental floss and some Iodine for the cut ends to prevent infection. The newbie Havanese mom will take over herself once she sees what is expected of her.

The length of labor will, of course, depend on the nunmber of the litter. If your Havanese mother takes a break in between contractions, you might want to assist the newborn pups in nursing from their mother during the intervals. The immune system of newborn puppies has not yet kicked in, and being able to take in the mother's first milk, or the colostrum, will pass on the mother's immunities to her pups - usually against diseases for which she had already been vaccinated.

Should there be any complications - a too-lengthy period of labor, a stuck puppy, or an insufficient number of placenta, you should call your veterinarian immediately. Have his number ready to hand during this process, for while you may not need to call him for a regular delivery, there is always the possibility of something going on.

So now the litter has been born, and your tired but accomplished Havanese mother should be allowed a period of rest. You will need to take good care of her and her puppies during the next few weeks - while she is lactating and as the puppies begin to grow.

Caring for and Weaning the Puppies

It is generally recommended that the dam should still be fed the same portions of food as in the last week of her diet - around two or three times more - to support her as she lactates. Should she be unable to adequately nurse her puppies - in cases of a very large litter of puppies, for example, then you should be ready to supplement this with puppy formula. Consult with your veterinarian regarding the recommended formula and the amount, as this would have to depend upon the weight of the puppies.

Puppies cannot regulate their own body temperature for the first few weeks, so they need to be kept warm. A chill is a very dangerous thing for a puppy to get. The box also needs to be kept clean - many breeders prefer to line the whelping box with newspapers which they can change as often as needed. The mother will stimulate them to urinate and defecate by rubbing their belles - but again, if the mother fails to do so, you can step in by using a cotton ball dipped in warm water.

Puppies' eyes open at about two weeks, and the ears at three. Before this, they are completely dependent on their mother and on you. Handle them gently, and also regularly, so that they become accustomed to your touch. They may also begin to stumble about on their legs and feet at this point.

Weaning begins at around two to four weeks, as you gradually begin to introduce them to more solid food. Always remember to go slowly, making small changes each day so as not to cause stomach upsets or indigestion. It is best to consult with a veterinarian so that you could discuss a feeding plan and schedule for the puppies.

Some prefer using puppy formula, others use dry puppy food soaked in water or broth. As the days and weeks pass, gradually increase the amount of food and decrease the amount of formula. Puppies should be fully weaned at around eight weeks, during which time they should already be pretty active and mobile. Socialization should also have begun at this time - with something as simple as getting them accustomed to your presence. You should already have brought them to the vet for their checkup and vaccinations.

Once fully weaned, at around the 7th to 12th week, they are finally ready to go to their new homes. This is the last phase of responsible breeding (though some breeders say it can last a lifetime), and it is no less important. Make sure that the puppies' new owners have the capacity to care for their new pet, with a good understanding of the breed and their unique needs and quirks.

Chapter Nine: Showing Your Havanese

The Havanese - charming, smart, funny and spirited dogs - seems almost naturally meant for show. Their long, silky hair for which they are known, and for which they have been dubbed as the Havana Silk Dog, is a delight to the eyes as well as to the touch. Even if you never enter your Havanese to any dog show, their diva-like nature somehow feels like they are at their own personal show.

If you are considering entering your Havanese in a dog show, it's important that you know more about the AKC Breed Standard for Havanese, as well as how to navigate your way through the world of shows. This chapter contains a condensed view of the AKC Havanese Breed Standard, as well as some tips and general advice on preparing your Havanese for show.

Havanese Breed Standard

General Appearance and Temperament - An outgoing, funny and intelligent. It is a small but sturdy breed, with a unique, springy gait and a playful, spirited personality.

Head and Neck - The skull of the head is broad and slightly rounded, with a moderate stop and flat cheeks. The neck is slightly arched.

Eyes and Ears - The eyes are large, dark brown and almond-shaped, with solid black rims except for chocolate dogs who may have somewhat lighter brown eyes and solid brown rims at the eyes. The ears are broad at the base, dropped, and with a distinct fold.

Body and Tail - The chest is deep and well-developed, and the entire body is slightly longer than the height at the withers. The tail is set high and arches up over the back, with a long, silky plume. A docked tail is cause for disqualification.

Legs, Feet and Gait - Elbows are tight to the body and forelegs are straight. The hind legs are muscular. The feet have arched toes and point straight ahead. The gait is springy.

Coat and Color - Any coat color and skin color is accepted. The coat itself is silky to the touch, soft and light in texture for both the outer and undercoat. This is long, abundant and wavy, flowing with movement but allows the natural lines of the dog to be seen. Causes for possible disqualification are a coarse, wiry coat and short coats, while flat, frizzy, single and curly coats are considered faults. Corded coats are allowed.

Temperament - Friendly, playful, intelligent and alert, sweet and non-quarrelsome.

Size - Ideally, the height should be from 9 to 10 1/2 inches, though 8 1/2 to 11 1/2 inches is also accepted.

Preparing Your Havanese for Show

The Havanese were only recently recognized by the AKC in 1996, but the popularity of this toy breed has grown steadily since then. But the preparation of your Havanese for show really should begin when they are puppies. Why? Aside from the necessary training and socialization, a Havanese show dog's coat must not be trimmed. And to maintain this full length of coat to show to full effect requires constant and daily grooming over a certain period of time. Corded coats, for instance, take about six months to train to cord. Coats kept naturally silky still need daily brushing and weekly baths, and that does not include the other grooming tasks for the eyes, teeth and nails.

Needless to say, your Havanese must also be trained, and again this is not something that can happen immediately. Though the Havanese is naturally intelligent and smart, it has been said that they can be challenging to housebreak. And of course, you would likely need to issue them certain commands during the show itself, as you go through the presentation and show your dog off to his best advantage.

That is why an intention to show your dog must be formed early - when they are still pups. The preparation begins in earnest from the time you bring them home and raise them.

If you think your Havanese has a good chance at the show, meeting all the conformation standards set by the AKC, then you can begin in earnest. Dog shows are usually held by the local kennel club nearest you, and they will have their own rules and regulations governing dog shows.

Do your research: get hold of their rules, examine the requirements, and see if you and your Havanese fit the bill. It might not be a bad idea either to visit one of these shows just to see what is happening, who are there, and which dog wins. This is also a magnificent time to network and build friendships with other Havanese owners. Bringing your Havanese along during these visits would also ensure that he becomes acclimated to the event and the great number of people and other dogs in a single location.o

Once you have decided to enter, here is a checklist of things that you should prepare for the big day:

- Registration papers and sufficient money for payment of required fees
- Food, water and snacks for you and your pet
- The necessary accessories such as a leash and collar, a crate with suitable beddings, and toys to keep him occupied during periods of waiting.
- Grooming supplies
- Medication, should this be needed by your dog

And don't forget that while this may, for some, be a competition, it is also a chance for you and your Havanese to have some fun!

Chapter Ten: Keeping Your Havanese Dog Healthy

For such a tiny dog, the Havanese are generally quite sturdy and healthy overall, with a pretty lengthy lifespan of some 14 to 16 years. They can be prone to certain health conditions, however, and information regarding these are provided below.

It is always good to remember that there will always be a potential for your Havanese to develop certain health conditions, regardless of how carefully the breeders have screened the parents, or how many health screenings and checks they may have undergone. Careful and responsible breeding minimizes the chances of diseases happening, but they are not a guarantee of complete health. Responsible breeders should be able to openly discuss with you any potential health problems that the Havanese breed may be prone to, including possible treatments, symptoms, and the like.

Being aware of these potential conditions is also useful for Havanese owners because early detection of the signs and symptoms of any of these health conditions will allow you to seek early medical help and treatment if such are available. Early detection of a disease in its early stages may mean that it can still be curable, and if not, at least it can be kept from getting any worse. Early and careful management of certain diseases may minimize the symptoms enough that your pet can still live a long and fruitful life.

In brief, the following are some of the more common health conditions affecting Havanese Dogs:

- Eye conditions such as cataracts and cherry eye
- Deafness

Common Health Problems Affecting Havanese Dogs

1. Eye Conditions

Cataracts

Cataracts result from the accumulation of protein in the eyes, which result in a cloudy or opaque lens. It can occur in either or both eyes, and may cause partial or complete vision loss. Be attentive for white, grey, light blue, or any abnormal coloration in the eyes. You may also notice that your Havanese is a little bit clumsy when he walks around; he may bump into things, or even bark at inanimate objects. These are signs that your Havanese may be having some difficulty with his eyesight.

There are different types of cataracts, though for the Havanese, the most common type is that which is genetic or congenital. It is possible, however, that the condition may be caused by other factors such as trauma, radiation exposure, diabetes, or simple ageing. There is no standard age for the onset of cataracts. It may be present at birth, after a few months, after a few years, or even in their later years.

At this time, there is still no test to screen for genetic or heritable cataracts, which is why there is a clamor for yearly eye testing on Havanese dogs. The difficulty is that the gene pool of the U.S.-bred Havanese is very small - only 11 original dogs that were brought to the U.S. from Cuba, so chances are good that most of their descendants are carriers of the gene. And because there is no test, and because cataracts can manifest at practically any age, you can never really be sure that the breeding stock is clean. Yearly eye testing seems to be the most feasible solution at present.

Should your Havanese start manifesting any of the symptoms above, it is imperative that you bring him to your veterinarian for a medical checkup. Proper diagnosis will be able to confirm if it is, indeed, cataracts. This is important because the symptoms are also similar to nuclear sclerosis, which is actually a normal condition of ageing and would not affect the eyesight at all. It would also help to rule out cataract development that happens as a result of diabetes mellitus, for which surgery is not advisable.

The reason why it is important to get a proper diagnosis, and as early as possible, is because hereditary cataracts, for as long as your pet is in good health, is actually treatable with surgery. If untreated or undiagnosed for too long, cataracts can cause progressive damage to the eye, ruling out surgery as a treatment should the condition worsen. Eventually, it can lead to painful inflammation, glaucoma, or even complete blindness.

Cherry Eye

Dogs have a third eyelid, otherwise called the nictitating membrane, and this helps to protect their eyes and to keep them moist through tear production. Cherry Eye happens when the gland in this membrane prolapses, or pops out of position, thus appearing like a pink or reddish "cherry-like protrusion" in the corner of the eye. Though not necessarily painful, irritation and inflammation may worsen the condition, and the longer exposure of the gland where it would be exposed to rubbing, may even lead to hemorrhage, and a permanent dry eye.

Cherry Eye is not per se genetic, though a Havanese may be predisposed to this condition if the connective tissue holding the gland in place is weak. It is this latter condition which may be genetic.

The most prevalent technique to correct this condition is a surgical procedure called the "pocket technique." A new pocket is made for the gland, where it is then tucked into and sewn into place. There are others who prefer nonsurgical treatment, which consists of medication combined with a gentle, downward massage that would pop the gland back into place. Recurrence is highly possible, so this might need to be repeated several times, though some claim that the massage can actually strenghten the connective muscles. In certain instances, the condition may even correct itself without any interference.

The most radical treatment possible is a surgical operation where the gland is completely removed. However, this had the unfortunate effect of causing "dry eye." With the removal of the tear gland, eye moisture and tear production is drastically reduced, thus compromising the health of the eye. Dry eye would then need to be treated for the rest of the pet's lifetime.

Deafness

This is another inherited condition, though it may also be caused by other factors such as infections. The good news is that there is a test (the Brainstem Auditory Evoked Response Test or BAER test) to diagnose this condition, and it is recommended that any Havanese older than 6 weeks be tested at least once in their lifetime. Doing so, coupled with responsible breeding, will at least minimize the chances of their passing it on to their offspring. In many instances, some owners may not even be aware that there is even any problem at all, and any offspring they produce will have a higher likelihood of also suffering from deafness.

Take note that the BAER test is not a test for the gene mutation itself. What it does is measure the auditory response in each ear to determine whether your Havanese can hear, or whether he is deaf. This is a very quick test and would not cause much discomfort to the pups.

Conditions that Affect Orthopedic Development

Patella Luxation

Although some instances of Patella Luxation are acquired conditions, it is strongly suspected that its manifestation in toy or miniature breeds is heritable.

In this instance, the kneecap or patella, which is part of the knee joint, luxates - or pops out of place, either towards the inside (medial position) or outside (lateral position) of the knee. When this happens, movement in the joint is inhibited, and there may be friction that can damage bone and joint tissues. It is a painful condition, and may cause some discomfort, or even lameness.

Because its incidence in Havanese dogs is mostly inherited, it can manifest early - as soon as when your puppy begins walking. You might notice an abnormal gait or stance, and a preference for carrying their weight on their front legs. On the other hand, should the cause be environmental, such as trauma of some kind, it can manifest even in later years, though there might already be some predisposition in the dog early on. A physical exam, coupled with an x-ray, will confirm if your Havanese has Patella Luxation.

Treatment may consist of surgery coupled with physical therapy.

Legg Perthes Disease

Sometimes also known as Legg-Calve-Perthes (LCP) disease, aseptic or avascular femoral head and neck necrosis, this is a condition which occurs mostly in miniature or toy breed dogs, manifesting sometime around 4 months to a year.

This condition affects the hip joints, where blood supply to the femoral head is cut off, thereby causing the death of the bone cells. When blood supply begins to flow back into the area, there is new bone growth that no longer fits the hip and joint conformation.

The early symptoms may be an abnormal gait, stiffness, or limping. This is also a painful condition so the Havanese may manifest some irritability during this time.

Confirmation of LCPD is by an x-ray, and some recommend requesting an LCPD check at the same time that your dog is being x-rayed for Hip Dysplasia, even if the test is not required for the breed. Because it will be read from the same x-ray, there should be no extra charge.

This is another inherited disease, though there is still no certainty as to how the gene is transmitted. Pay attention to limited movements in your Havanese, difficulty walking, or a sudden lameness from regular activities that do not seem to get better after a reasonable time.

Treatment depends on the severity of the disease - which can range from mild to severe. Mild cases are usually prescribed with anti-inflammatory medication and a period of rest or limited activity. The more severe cases, on the other hand, would require surgery wherein the part of the bone causing the discomfort is removed. Prognosis is generally good, and there is a good possibility for complete recovery after recuperation coupled with therapy.

Hip Dysplasia

Hip Dysplasia occurs when there is a laxity or looseness in the hip joint, leading to subluxation or partial dislocation of the hip joints. If left unletreated for too long, it may eventually lead to osteoarthritis and other degenerative bone changes.

This is another inherited condition, and while it is more common in larger dog breeds, has not been unheard of among certain small dog breeds such as the Havanese.

Watch out for signs of limping, a certain difficulty or slowness in rising or moving, bunny-like hopping in the hind legs, or a reluctance to walk and play. Confirmation of the presence of Hip Dysplasia is by an x-ray, and treatment also depends on the severity of the condition. Sometimes limited or controlled exercise, coupled with anti-inflammatory medicine may be enough. If the condition is very severe, surgery is also an option.

Conditions that Affect Major Organs

Liver Shunt

The liver works by clearing toxins from the blood. When blood bypasses the liver and enters the bloodstream unfiltered, it can lead to a host of problems such as damage to tissues and some of the major internal organs. This is because the unfiltered blood may still contain some harmful toxins that can poison tissues and cells inside the body.

This can occur at an early age, before the puppies reach one year, and the signs and symptoms are wide-ranging. Some of the symptoms to watch out for are disorientation, depression, compulsive pacing or circling, poor weight gain, sleeplessness, vomiting, seizures, and even temporary blindness. Since the liver is responsible for various functions such as circulation, detoxification, metabolism, temperate regulation, and waste removal, many of these functions can therefore be compromised by this condition.

Fortunately, most instances of Liver Shunt in toy dog breeds are extrahepatic, which is operable, and can therefore be resolved with surgery. Prognosis for recovery is generally good.

Heart Disease

Heart disease is another condition which seems to manifest in some Havanese. This usually involves weakend hearts that cannot efficiently supply blood to the body and its organs. While dogs do not have heart attacks per se, they may develop congestive heart failure, which is fatal. The problem is that while the dog may develop the condition at an early age, some of the symptoms may not manifest until several years later, when the disease is already severe.

Some of the symptoms include sudden weight loss, coughing, fatigue or lethargy, shortness of breath, poor appetite, a reluctance to exercise, and fainting. Bring your Havanese to a veterinarian if this happens, and the earlier the better. The sooner the diagnosis, the earlier the treatment - which may consist of prescribed medications.

Preventing Illness with Vaccinations

A rabies vaccination is the only one that is legally required for dogs, but there are a host of other vaccinations that can help to protect your Havanese from contracting certain illnesses or diseases, which they may get from the environment or from other dogs or animals.

It is good to have a discussion with your vet to determine which vaccinations to give your Havanese, and at what intervals. Many times, this would depend upon the prevalence of certain illnesses in your region, so there is no real standard or definitive guide that would be true for all regions and for all breeds. Such a discussion with your vet is also important given the recent outbreak of opinions that not all vaccinations and booster shots are good for dogs, and some may even have unfortunate side-effects. But how do you draw the line against over-vaccinating your Havanese, versus leaving them unprotected? Your Vet should at least be able to give you recommendations of necessary specific vaccines depending on the prevalence of diseases in your area.

Below is a table providing a general vaccination schedule for dogs. Again, remember that this is only a guide, and the specific needs of your Havanese would vary depending on your region.

Vaccination Schedule for Havanese	
Age	Vaccine
5 weeks	Parvovirus
6-8 weeks	Adenovirus, Distemper, Hepatitis, Parainfluenza, Parvovirus
12 weeks	Rabies and Leptospirosis
14 weeks	Lyme Disease and Leptospirosis
16 weeks	Leptospirosis

Havanese Care Sheet

If you don't have time to go through the entire book, but are in search of specific information regarding your Havanese, then this section is for you. Following is a quick summary of some of the more common information and facts regarding Havanese dogs, broken down into the following sections; Basic Havanese Information, habitat requirements, nutritional needs, and breeding information.

These can be read over at a quick glance, but don't forget to check back whenever you can for a more comprehensive discussion regarding the information you are looking for in the preceding sections.

1.) Basic Havanese Information

Pedigree: Bichon Tenerife, *Blanquito de la Habana* ("little white dog of Havana"), Poodle, Barbet

AKC Group: Toy Group

Types: no distinction

Breed Size: small

Height: 23-27 cm (9-11 inches)

Weight: 7-14 lbs (3-6 kg)

Coat Length: Long, slightly wavy, profuse and undulating, ranging from 6-8 inches

Coat Texture: very soft double coat, lightweight and silky; in some instances, the undercoat is absent;

Color: all colors possible, including white, cream, fawn, red, chocolate brown, beige, gold, silver, blue, and black, either a solid color or a combination (e.g., sable, brindle, black and tan, tri-color, Irish pied, parti-colored, belton, piebald, black and white, beige black, and white

Eyes and Nose: dark brown eyes with almond-shaped lids surrounded by black pigment; black nose, though chocolate brown dogs may have dark brown pigment on their nose

Ears: dropped and folded ears that can reach halfway to the nose when extended

Tail: arched forward and carried up over its back

Temperament: loyal and attached to their owners, active and lively, very friendly, very sociable, loves to perform in front of others, great need for affection, loves attention, people-oriented, peaceful and gentle

Strangers: friendly even to strangers, though may be a bit shy

Other Dogs: friendly with other dogs

Other Pets: friendly with other pets

Training: very smart and easily trained

Exercise Needs: average, daily exercise can be met with a good game session or a short walk, for about 20-40 minutes a day.

Health Conditions: Eye Conditions such as cataracts, cherry eye,

Luxating patella, liver disease, heart disease, cataracts, retinal dysplasia, tear stains, progressive retinal atrophy, poodle eye, juvenile heritable characters, chonrdodysplasia, leg-calve perthes disease, cardiac, liver and kidney problems, unilateral and bilateral deafness, sebacious adentis, seizures, and dry skin

Lifespan: average 12 to 14 years

2.) Habitat Requirements

Recommended Accessories: crate, dog bed, food/water dishes, treats, toys, collar, leash, identification tag, harness, grooming supplies

Collar and Harness: sized by weight

Grooming Supplies: slicker, bristle or steel pin brush, 2-in-1 comb, shedding blade, liquid detangler or baby oil

Grooming Frequency: brush several times a week, clipping or trimming when desired

Energy Level: very high, originally bred as a hunting retriever dog

Exercise Requirements: about 20-40 minutes of exercise per day

Crate: highly recommended

Crate Size: just large enough for dog to lie down and turn around comfortably

Crate Extras: lined with blanket or plush pet bed

Food/Water: stainless steel or ceramic bowls, clean daily

Toys: start with an assortment, see what the dog likes; include some mentally stimulating toys

Exercise Ideas: agility exercises on standard obstacle courses, fly-ball, jumping or dancing,

3.) Nutritional Needs

Nutritional Needs: water, protein, carbohydrate, fats, vitamins, minerals

RER: 30(body weight in kilograms) + 70

Calorie Needs: varies by age, weight, and activity level; RER modified with activity level

Amount to Feed: 1/2 to 1 cup of high quality dry food a day, divided into two meals

Important Ingredients: fresh animal protein (chicken, beef, lamb, turkey, eggs), digestible carbohydrates (rice, oats, barley), animal fats

Important Minerals: calcium, phosphorus, potassium, magnesium, iron, copper and manganese

Important Vitamins: Vitamin A, Vitamin A, Vitamin B-12, Vitamin D, Vitamin C

Look For: AAFCO statement of nutritional adequacy; protein at top of ingredients list; no artificial flavors, dyes, preservatives

4.) Breeding Information

Age of First Heat: around 6 months, sometimes earlier or later

Heat (Estrus) Cycle: 14 to 21 days

Frequency: twice a year, every 6 to 7 months

Greatest Fertility: 11 to 15 days into the cycle

Gestation Period: 59 to 63 days

Pregnancy Detection: possible after 21 days, best to wait 28-30 days before exam

Feeding Pregnant Dogs: maintain normal diet until week 5 or 6 then slightly increase rations by 20 to 50 percent for the last five weeks

Signs of Labor: body temperature drops below normal 100° to 102°F (37.7° to 38.8°C), may be as low as 98°F (36.6°C); dog begins nesting in a dark, quiet place

Contractions: *ten to thirty minutes, in waves of an hour or so each time*

Whelping: *may last anywhere from a few hours to half a day or more*

Puppies: *born with eyes and ears closed; eyes open at 3 weeks, teeth develop at 10 weeks*

Litter Size: average 1-9 puppies

Size at Birth: 4-7 oz.

Weaning: supplement with controlled portions of moistened puppy food at 3-5 weeks, with water freely available, fully weaned at 5-6 weeks

Socialization: start as early as possible to prevent puppies from being nervous as an adult, preferably before 14-16 weeks of age

Index

R

S

T

Photo Credits

Cover Photo by buchsammy via Pixabay.com.
<https://pixabay.com/en/dog-flare-havanese-pet-outdoor-1134493/>

Page 1 Photo by office174 via Pixabay.com.
<https://pixabay.com/en/dog-havanese-good-view-animal-pet-929044/>

Page 7 Photo by Csilva via Wikimedia Commons.
<https://commons.wikimedia.org/wiki/File:Havanes-brazil.jpg>

Page 15 Photo by Edumegina via Wikimedia Commons.
<https://commons.wikimedia.org/wiki/File:Havaneser_Anton_crop.jpg>

Page 25 Photo by JGKatz via Wikimedia Commons.
<https://commons.wikimedia.org/wiki/File:The_Havanese.tif>

Page 37 Photo by Scheepers100 via Wikimedia Commons.
<https://commons.wikimedia.org/wiki/File:Havanezer_Tail whispers.JPG>

Page 41 Photo by IlonaRieck via Wikimedia Commons.
<https://commons.wikimedia.org/wiki/File:Rickys_Estelle_Ave_Maria_with_her_mother_Emmeli_%28VDH_-_Zucht%29.jpg>

Page 51 Photo by Bagienny via Wikimedia Commons. <https://commons.wikimedia.org/wiki/File:Bichon_havanese _cezar.jpg>

Page 61 Photo by Petra Behr via Wikimedia Commons. <https://commons.wikimedia.org/wiki/File:Aragorn_von_de r_wolfspfote.jpg>

Page 71 Photo by Loganandgarth via Wikimedia Commons. <https://commons.wikimedia.org/wiki/File:Havanese_puppi es_cd2.jpg>

Page 81 Photo by audrey_sel via Wikimedia Commons, as uploaded by Frei sein. <https://commons.wikimedia.org/wiki/File:A_Havanese_jud ging.jpg>

Page 87 Photo by Томасина via Wikimedia Commons. <https://commons.wikimedia.org/wiki/File:Bichon_Havanais _Pair.JPG>

Page 99 Photo by buchsammy via Pixabay.com. <https://pixabay.com/en/dog-flare-havanese-pet-outdoor-1134492/>

References

"BAER - hearing test." havaneseabc.com.
   <http://www.havaneseabc.com/baer.html>

"Basic Havanese Puppy Grooming." Paula Martel.
   <http://www.havanesefanciers.com/basic_puppy_grooming>

"Bichon." Wikipedia. <https://en.wikipedia.org/wiki/Bichon>

"Bichon Breeds." Catherine Marien-de Luca.
   <http://dogbreeds.bulldoginformation.com/bichon-type-dogs.html>

"Bringing Home Your New Dog." dogtime.
   <http://dogtime.com/dog-health/general/262-adults-bringing-home>

"Canine Nutrition Basics." Claudia Kawczynska.
   <http://thebark.com/content/canine-nutrition-basics>

"Cataracts in Dogs." vetary.com.
   <https://www.vetary.com/dog/condition/cataracts>

"Cherry Eye." Wikipedia.
   <https://en.wikipedia.org/wiki/Cherry_eye>

"Clicker Training Basics." Havanese Fanciers of Canada.
   <http://www.havanesefanciers.com/clickertraining>

"Current Costs of First Year Havanese Puppy Ownership."
Holly Mastroianni.
<http://www.prweb.com/releases/royalflushhavanesepu
ppies/dogcostfirstyear/prweb11101502.htm>

"Dog Heat Cycle and Breeding." Kelly Roper.
<http://dogs.lovetoknow.com/wiki/Dog_Heat_Cycle_and
_Breeding>

"Dog Mating Concerns and Procedures." Kelly Roper.
<http://dogs.lovetoknow.com/wiki/Dogs_Mating>

"Dog Nutrition Tips." ASPCA. <http://www.aspca.org/pet-
care/dog-care/dog-nutrition-tips>

"Dog Reproduction (The Heat Cycle)." Dog Breed Info
Center.
<http://www.dogbreedinfo.com/breedingheat.htm>

"Eye Testing." HavaneseABC's.
<http://www.havaneseabc.com/cerf.html>

"Feeding Your Havanese." hfc.
<http://www.havanesefanciers.com/feeding>

"Genetics: Eye Problems." hfc.
<http://www.havanesefanciers.com/genetic_eyeproblems
>

"Grooming the pet Havanese." Havanese ABC's.
<http://www.havaneseabc.com/grooming.html>

"Havanese." Animal World. <http://dogs.animal-world.com/Toy-Dog-Breeds/Havanese.php#Availability>

"Havanese." nylabone.com. <http://www.nylabone.com/dog-101/dog-breeds/havanese/>

"Havanese." vetstreet.com. <http://www.vetstreet.com/dogs/havanese#health>

"Havanese." Wikipedia. <https://en.wikipedia.org/wiki/Havanese#History>

"Havanese ABC's." Havanese ABC's. <http://www.havaneseabc.com/ABC.html>

"Havanese Dog Breed Information Including History." Elive Havanese. <http://www.elitehavanese.com/havanese.html>

"Havanese Health." The Havanese Club of America, Inc. <http://www.havanese.org/health>

"Havanese Health Issues." Havanese Club of America, Inc. <http://www.havanese.org/education/new-owners/78-havanese-health-issues>

"Havanese History." Havanese Club of America, Inc. <http://www.havanese.org/about/history>

"Havanese Puppies." ErasHavanese. <http://erashavanese.com/havanese-puppies/>

"Havanese - Temperament & Personality." petwave.com. <http://www.petwave.com/Dogs/Breeds/Havanese/Personality.aspx>

"Hereditary and Genetic Disorders of the Havanese Breed." Havanese ABC's. <http://www.havaneseabc.com/genetics.html>

"Hip Dysplasia." Penny Will. <http://www.havanesefanciers.com/hipdysplasia>

"Hip Dysplasia: Causes, Diagnoses, Treatments." Brandy Arnold. <http://www.dogingtonpost.com/hip-dysplasia-causes-diagnoses-treatments/>

"Housebreaking and Litter Training." Havanese Fanciers of Canada. <http://www.havanesefanciers.com/housebreaking>

"House Training a Puppy." ErasHavanese. <http://erashavanese.com/house-training-a-puppy/>

"House Training Issues." Talemaker Havanese. <http://www.talemakerhavanese.com/house-training-issues/>

"How Much Dog Food Should I Feed My Puppy?" Carlotta Cooper. <http://dogfood.guru/how-much-dog-food-should-i-feed-my-puppy/>

"How to Choose Your Havanese Puppy." editorialtoday.com.

<http://www.streetdirectory.com/etoday/how-to-choose-your-havanese-puppy-ufwlfl.html>

"How to Puppy proof Home." Faust House Havanese.
<http://www.fausthousehavanese.org/how-to-puppy-proof-your-home.html>

"Info about Havanese." Indiana Havanese Puppies.
<http://www.indianahavanesepups.com/info.htm>

"Introducing the Clicker to Your Havanese." Claire.
<http://www.havanesefanciers.com/introtoclickertraining>

"Is It Right For You?" Mimosa Havanese.
<http://www.havaneseabc.com/choice.html>

"LCPD: Legg-Calve Perthes Disease." Penny Will.
<http://www.havanesefanciers.com/LCPD>

"Official Standard of the Havanese." AKC.
<http://images.akc.org/pdf/breeds/standards/Havanese.pdf?_ga=1.157119288.2096669137.1462463644>

"Patella Luxation." Penny Will.
<http://www.havanesefanciers.com/patellarluxation>

"Pregnancy Guide: Prenatal Care, Whelping and Raising Puppies." Dog Breed Info Center.
<http://www.dogbreedinfo.com/breedingpregnancyguide.htm>

"Prolapsed Gland of the Third Eyelid ("Cherry Eye"). Northwest Animal Eye Specialists. <http://www.northwestanimaleye.com/cherry-eye.pml>

"Puppy proofing your Home." Leslie. <http://www.havaneseforum.com/8-puppy-area/8804-puppy-proofing-your-home.html>

"Puppy Proofing Your Home and Yard." nevenahavanese.com. <http://www.nevenahavanese.com/Puppy-Proofing-Home.html>

"Responsible Breeding." AKC. <http://www.akc.org/dog-breeders/responsible-breeding>

"Should Sassy Have Puppies?" Dog Owner's Guide. <http://www.canismajor.com/dog/hvpup1.html>

"Showing Your Havanese." terrificpets.com. <http://www.terrificpets.com/articles/102193565.asp>

"Small Breed Dog Food." Carlotta Cooper. <http://dogfood.guru/small-breed/>

"Socialization of Your Havanese." Mylad Havanese. <http://www.myladhavanese.com/Socialization%20of%20Havanese.asp>

"The Havase Liver Shunt." terrificpets.com. <http://www.terrificpets.com/articles/102195965.asp>

"The Luxating Knee." Orthopedic Foundation for Animals.
   <http://www.offa.org/pl_overview.html>

"Training." Stony Sun Kennels.
   <http://www.havanese.ca/Training_your_havanese.htm>

"Training Myths." Mimosa Havanese.
   <http://www.havaneseabc.com/multidiscipline.html>

"Vaccination." Havanese ABC's.
   <http://www.havaneseabc.com/vaccination.html>

"What is the Best Dog Food For a Havanese?" Carlotta
   Cooper. <http://dogfood.guru/what-is-the-best-dog-food-
   for-a-havanese/>

Feeding Baby
Cynthia Cherry
978-1941070000

Axolotl
Lolly Brown
978-0989658430

Dysautonomia, POTS
Syndrome
Frederick Earlstein
978-0989658485

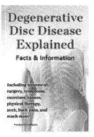

Degenerative Disc
Disease Explained
Frederick Earlstein
978-0989658485

Sinusitis, Hay Fever,
Allergic Rhinitis Explained
Frederick Earlstein
978-1941070024

Wicca
Riley Star
978-1941070130

Zombie Apocalypse
Rex Cutty
978-1941070154

Capybara
Lolly Brown
978-1941070062

Eels As Pets
Lolly Brown
978-1941070167

Scabies and Lice Explained
Frederick Earlstein
978-1941070017

Saltwater Fish As Pets
Lolly Brown
978-0989658461

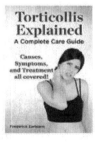

Torticollis Explained
Frederick Earlstein
978-1941070055

Kennel Cough
Lolly Brown
978-0989658409

Physiotherapist, Physical
Therapist
Christopher Wright
978-0989658492

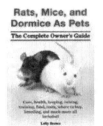

Rats, Mice, and Dormice
As Pets
Lolly Brown
978-1941070079

Wallaby and Wallaroo Care
Lolly Brown
978-1941070031

Bodybuilding Supplements
Explained
Jon Shelton
978-1941070239

Demonology
Riley Star
978-19401070314

Pigeon Racing
Lolly Brown
978-1941070307

Dwarf Hamster
Lolly Brown
978-1941070390

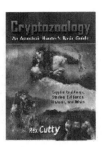

Cryptozoology
Rex Cutty
978-1941070406

Eye Strain
Frederick Earlstein
978-1941070369

Inez The Miniature Elephant
Asher Ray
978-1941070353

Vampire Apocalypse
Rex Cutty
978-1941070321

39063029R00077

Made in the USA
Middletown, DE
03 January 2017